Botanical Illustration

Kristina Mercedes Urquhart

✳ Smithsonian

© 2019 Smithsonian Institution. The name "Smithsonian" and the Smithsonian logo are registered trademarks owned by the Smithsonian Institution.

Contributing Author

Allison Duarte, M.A.

Consultants

Tamieka Grizzle, Ed.D.
K–5 STEM Lab Instructor
Harmony Leland Elementary School

Alice Tangerini
Staff Illustrator
Smithsonian

Publishing Credits

Rachelle Cracchiolo, M.S.Ed., *Publisher*
Conni Medina, M.A.Ed., *Managing Editor*
Diana Kenney, M.A.Ed., NBCT, *Content Director*
Véronique Bos, *Creative Director*
June Kikuchi, *Content Director*
Robin Erickson, *Art Director*
Seth Rogers, *Editor*
Mindy Duits, *Senior Graphic Designer*
Smithsonian Science Education Center

Image Credits: front cover, p.1 Jeff Malet Photography/Newscom; p.4 Daniel Berehulak/Getty Images; p.6 (left), p.14, p.17 (all), p.20, p.25 (bottom), p.26, pp.26–27 (background), p.27 (top), 27 (bottom) © Smithsonian; p.7 (insert) Courtesy of Mervi Hjelmroos-Koski, Ph.D., D.Sc.; p.8 (bottom right) Bridgeman Images; p.9 (center) Wellcome Images; p.10 (left) Natural History Museum, London, UK/Bridgeman Images; p.10 (right) Linnean Society, London, UK/Bridgeman Images; p.11, p.12 (left) Public domain; p.12 (right) Bibliotheque des Arts Decoratifs, Paris, France/Archives Charmet/Bridgeman Images; p.13 (left) Fotosearch/Getty Images; p.13 (right) The Natural History Museum/Alamy; p.24 Photo by Donna Calcavecchio, courtesy of Wendy Hollender; p.25 (top) Photo by Carol Woodin, courtesy of Wendy Hollender; all other images from iStock and/or Shutterstock.

Library of Congress Cataloging-in-Publication Data

Names: Urquhart, Kristina Mercedes, author.
Title: Botanical illustration / Kristina Mercedes Urquhart.
Description: Huntington Beach, CA : Teacher Created Materials, [2018] | Audience: K to grade 3. | Includes index.
Identifiers: LCCN 2017060491 (print) | LCCN 2017061411 (ebook) | ISBN 9781493869237 (e-book) | ISBN 9781493866830 (pbk.)
Subjects: LCSH: Botanical illustration--Juvenile literature. | Plants--Drawings--Juvenile literature.
Classification: LCC QK98.2 (ebook) | LCC QK98.2 .U77 2018 (print) | DDC 580.22/2--dc23
LC record available at https://lccn.loc.gov/2017060491

Smithsonian

© 2019 Smithsonian Institution. The name "Smithsonian" and the Smithsonian logo are registered trademarks owned by the Smithsonian Institution.

Teacher Created Materials

5301 Oceanus Drive
Huntington Beach, CA 92649-1030
www.tcmpub.com

ISBN 978-1-4938-6683-0
© 2019 Teacher Created Materials, Inc.

Table of Contents

Bringing Nature to Life

Have you ever drawn a plant that you saw in real life? Did you make sure that you included every leaf, stem, and flower that you saw? Was your work **accurate** down to the smallest detail? Then a job as a botanical illustrator might be a good fit for you. These artists have a big job to do. They draw pictures of plants with lots of details. The plants almost come to life on the pages.

Botany is the field of science that studies plants. It is a huge field of study. There are a lot of plants in the world! An illustrator is someone whose job is to draw. Botanical illustrators draw plants for their jobs.

These drawings are used in different ways. Some people use them to teach about plants around the world. Others put them on display in museum **exhibits**.

A woman observes botanical art in a museum.

A woman draws flowers in a garden.

Botanical illustrations are very detailed.

Tafel 46.

1. Blutkraut, Lythrum salicaria.
2. Portel, Peplis portula.

Botanical illustrations can be drawn in black and white. They can also be drawn in color. It all depends on what style the artist chooses. Black and white drawings show more detail. Color helps the art come to life. Artists decide what is best for each drawing.

Many drawings are on plain white backgrounds. They include scale measurements of the plants. Scale is the size of something compared to something else. Parts of the plants may be drawn close-up to show more of the plants' parts. Other drawings have backgrounds. They show what plants look like in their natural landscapes.

All the drawings show parts of plants, such as the roots, stems, leaves, buds, flowers, and fruit. The drawings are used to help scientists learn more about plants.

Artists choose whether to use color or leave art in black and white.

Big libraries called archives (AHR-kyvz) store botanical illustrations. That way, they are easier to find.

Drawing on the Past

People have drawn plants for thousands of years. All over the world, people made **records** of plants by drawing them. There were no computers or cameras long ago. Drawing was the only way to remember important plants.

Before there was bottled medicine, people used plants to heal their bodies. People put plants on bug bites, cuts, and bruises. People dried plants, too. They were made into teas. The teas were used as medicine. People were able to stay healthy by drinking teas made from these special plants.

Plants used in this way are medicinal (meh-DIH-sih-nuhl). That means they help heal people who are hurt or sick. They were very important. They were the first plants that **botanists** recorded.

People use plants to make medicine.

Two men illustrate plants in the 1500s.

Mint is an **herb** used by people to make stomach pain go away. It tastes great, too!

The oldest botanical drawings are over 4,000 years old. That is really old! They were found in ancient (AYN-chihnt) Egyptian tombs and temples. The Greeks and Romans drew plants, too. They painted plants on pottery and coins. Plant drawings were put in books called herbals (UHR-buhlz). These books were about plants that heal. Herbals made it easier to find special plants when they were needed.

Age of Discovery

Explorers traveled the world to see what they could find. They made drawings of the plants they found. They wanted to have records of these new **species**. They took seeds and living plants home with them, too.

In the 1700s, explorers found many new plants. There was a rush to draw all the new plants. The world needed botanical illustrators.

Explorers collected plants on trips and later recorded them in books.

Going Back in Time

Some botanical illustrators draw plants that are now extinct. That means they do not exist anymore. Artists work with **fossils** to make drawings of what these plants looked like when they were alive. Some fossils are not complete. Others do not show many of the plant's details. To draw from fossils, artists have to combine what they already know about plants with what they see.

Alexander von Humboldt was an explorer who collected and recorded many plants.

Drawing Styles

There are two styles of botanical illustration. The first is called the Linnaean (lih-NAY-uhn) style. It is named after the man who created it: Carl Linnaeus. As a young boy, he loved plants. He had his own garden by the time he was five years old. Linnaeus could name almost every plant he saw. He grew up to be a teacher and botanist.

In this style of drawing, plants have a lot of detail. They have beautiful colors. The background is white. The important parts of the plant are large so that they are easy to see.

Carl Linnaeus

Linnaean style art

At the time of his death, Linnaeus was one of the most famous scientists in Europe.

In 1739, William Bartram was born. He loved nature and grew up to be a botanist and an artist. He was a poet, too. Most importantly, he was a naturalist. He shared what he knew about nature by teaching others about it.

Bartram created a new style of drawing plants. It is called the ecological (ee-kuh-LAW-jih-kuhl) style. This style looks at all of nature, not just the plants. Drawings include the animals and bugs that live with plants.

ecological style art

William Bartram

Make Your Mark

Today, botanical illustrators are **hired** to draw plants for scientists. Botanists spend a lot of time studying plants. Drawings help them show what they've learned.

The most important part of an illustrator's job is to make their drawings accurate. That means they should look just like the plants do in real life. Every detail must be right.

Drawings must show the parts of the plants that help make new plants. They must show special parts that make the plants stand out from others that are similar. They also must show the way plants grow and change over time. Some plants grow tall and strong. Others stay low to the ground and make a clump. This is the plant's *habit*. Even though each plant grows a little differently, all plants of the same kind have the same habit.

Botanical illustrator Alice Tangerini works on an illustration.

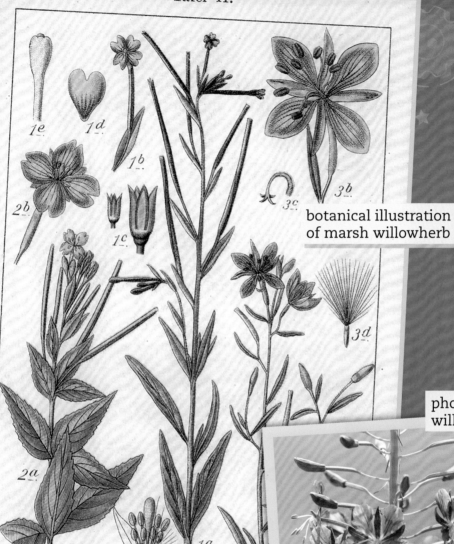

1a 1e 1d 1b 2b 1c 3c 3b 3d 2a 2c 1a

botanical illustration of marsh willowherb

photo of marsh willowherb

1. Sumpfröschen, Epilobium palustr
2. Dreikantiges Weidenröschen, E. t
3. Fleischer-Röschen, E. Fleischeri.

One plant illustration can take almost 50 hours to draw!

Botanical artists work together with the scientists who hire them. The scientist's job is to write the text that describes the plant. The artist's job is to make a drawing that will give that text more meaning. Both jobs are equal.

First, scientists and artists try to identify the plant by looking at it. If they can't identify the plant, they look at other plants that are similar. This helps them know what parts the plant has and what details need to be pointed out. Then, they classify the plant. Scientists have special **categories** for each type of plant. Artists use the text to help them draw the plant. If the plant does not have a name, scientists name the plant.

Plant Identification

Identify: *Sunflower*

Describe: *bright yellow petals around a large, brown seed disc; heart-shaped leaves; 5-foot-tall stem; blooms annually*

Classify: *Helianthus family*

Name: *Helianthus annuus*

dried leaves

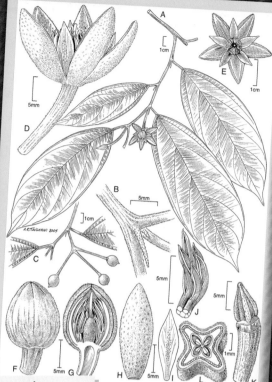

Botanical illustrations make details easy to see.

Plants Are Pretty

Like all artists, botanical illustrators think about the elements of drawing when working on a piece. These elements include:

- **line:** Should the lines be thick or thin? Light or dark?

- **shape:** Should the drawing be two-dimensional (2-D) or three-dimensional (3-D)?

- **tone:** How should the drawing be shaded?

- **space:** How much of the space around the plant should be included?

- **color:** Should the drawing be in color? Should it be black and white?

Botanical illustrators must follow some rules. These rules help make all plant drawings easy to compare. This way, people from around the world can understand the drawings, even if they speak different languages!

Here are some rules of botanical illustration:

1. Do not draw too many shadows. (They block out details.)

2. Use dots to create depth and show a plant's shape. (Depth is a sense of space.)

3. Light should appear to come from the top left side of a drawing. (This helps compare plants because shadows are all on the same side.)

4. Keep drawings accurate.

5. Botanical illustrators need to know everything about plants they draw and their parts. (This is called structure. The structure of the plant is how all the parts come together.)

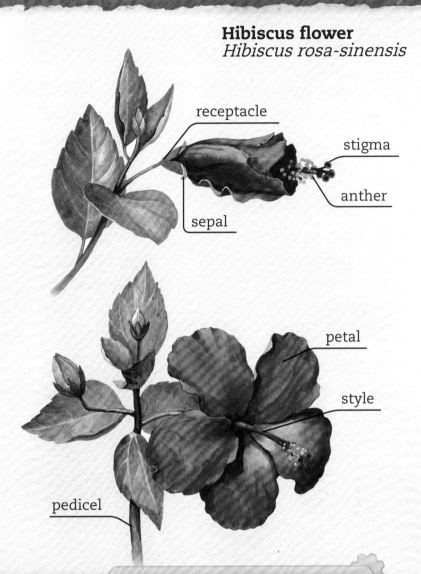

Hibiscus flower
Hibiscus rosa-sinensis

receptacle

stigma

anther

sepal

petal

style

pedicel

Tools of the Trade

Today, many botanical illustrators use computers to draw. But simple tools work well, too. Botanical illustrators use ink pens to draw outlines and add depth. They use **graphite** pencils to add shading. They use brushes made from animal hairs to draw smooth curved lines. Finally, they use pencils or watercolors to add color.

The Right Stuff

To get a piece just right, botanical illustrators need to look closely at real plants. Once they have plants to study, it is important that they use the right tools to make the best illustrations that they can.

Plant Materials

Plant samples can be live or dried. Most of the time, artists work from dried plants. These plants have been preserved. That means they have been kept looking the same as when they were alive. Dried plants are stored in plant banks called herbaria (uhr-BEHR-ee-uh).

Artists draw from living plants, too. Some plants come straight from the garden! Some artists are also gardeners. They grow their own plants to use as **subjects**. Other artists travel the world to find their next subjects.

preserved samples in an herbarium

Plant Preservation

Have you ever put a flower between the pages of a book to let it dry? Scientists and artists do something similar to preserve plants. First, they find plants they want to dry. Then, they put them in a machine called a plant press. It looks like a stack of wood and paper with straps around it. Plants are placed between sheets of paper and cardboard. This helps **absorb** moisture. When plants are fully dried, they are ready to be stored.

Botanical Art Materials

Artists need good drawing tools. The best tools help artists be precise. Precise means "exact." Illustrators are very good at this!

Art pencils are some of the best tools to start sketching. These are like the pencils you use in school. But these pencils come in a number of different shades of gray. They are great for sketching. They can be sharpened and erased easily. Artists also use colored pencils. Artists can use them to add color quickly without waiting for ink or paint to dry.

Some artists use tools other than pencils. One of these tools is a special pen called a dip pen. It gets that name because you must dip it in a jar of ink to use it. The artist may also use a quill, which is the pointy end of a feather. Watercolor painting is another way to add color and detail. The artist mixes the colors and paints them with a brush.

quill in ink

watercolor painting

MATHEMATICS

Shrink It

Many artists measure the plants they draw. This helps them keep their artwork in **proportion**. If they draw a plant half its normal height, then they also draw it half its normal width. This is called drawing to scale.

Modern Technology

Artists use many tools. Pencils, pens, and brushes are some of them. These are traditional tools. They have been used for a long time. Modern tools, such as computers, are used, too.

Botanical artists practice for many years. Most start out with pencils. Then, they move on to paint. Some learn how to draw on tablet computers with special pens. There are special programs just for drawing. They allow artists to erase and add color, just like they can with pencils and paper. Unlike paper, however, you can use a tablet over and over again. Sketches can be saved on the tablet instead of in drawers.

Botanical artists can use traditional tools, modern tools, or a mix of both. But the goal is still the same. They want to make a plant come to life through art.

This woman uses a computer to draw.

Botanical illustrator Wendy Hollender uses pencils and colored pencils to draw a peanut plant.

Scientific illustrators also work in other areas of science. Some draw living animals, such as insects, or even extinct animals, such as dinosaurs.

25

The Need for Botanical Illustrators

Keeping records is an important part of science. People can learn from records that have been saved. Botanical illustrators work with scientists to make records of all of the plants they find. These records help pass on what we know about plants. Future scientists can learn from these records and add to them. One day, some of the plants that have been drawn may become extinct. People will not be able to go and look at the plant in the wild anymore. The record will be all that is left.

Studying extinct plants and animals may help in the future. People can use these records to learn about what caused plants to die. And they may find ways to protect the plants that are still around. Drawings that are being made today can help people in the future.

Tangerini draws a plant outside.

This drawing shows what life may have looked like millions of years ago.

This illustrator draws underwater!

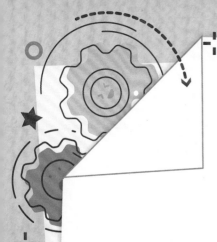

STEAM CHALLENGE

Define the Problem

Sometimes, botanical illustrators preserve plants before they draw them. Other times, they go to the plants in nature. You have been asked to make an illustration of a plant in your neighborhood. Your task is to find the best way to get a detailed drawing of your specimen that is easily identified by someone else.

 Constraints: The plant must be drawn with the specimen in front of you and not from memory.

 Criteria: Draw a plant using as many details as you can to help a partner identify the plant.

Research and Brainstorm

Where do artists find plants? How do artists collect specimens? What are the pros and cons to collecting a specimen? What are the pros and cons to drawing a specimen in the field?

Design and Build

Make a detailed plan for how you will draw your plant. Will you draw it outside where it is growing? What materials and tools will you use to draw it? Then, follow your plan and make your drawing.

Test and Improve

After making your illustration, show it to a partner. Can they identify the plant? How can you improve it? Modify your plan, and try again.

Reflect and Share

Think about your experience. What went well? What did not?

Glossary

absorb—to take in or soak up something, usually a liquid

accurate—free from mistakes or errors

botanists—people who work in a branch of biology that studies plants

categories—groups that include similar things

exhibits—public shows, usually for art

explorers—people who travel to discover new places

fossils—traces or prints of the remains of plants or animals preserved in earth or rock

graphite—a gray mineral that leaves marks on surfaces; used inside pencils

herb—a type of plant with a strong smell and taste, used for cooking, perfume, and medicine

hired—given work in exchange for money

proportion—having the correct shape and being the correct distance apart

records—documents that tell about past events

species—a group of plants or animals that are similar and can produce young

subjects—things that are the focus of study

Index

Do you want to draw nature?
Here are some tips to get you started.

"To me, all plants are works of art. Capturing their beauty on paper is challenging, but I can't imagine doing anything else! When I was a child, I used to draw the birds and insects I saw in our backyard. Draw every chance you get!" —**Alice Tangerini, Illustrator**

"Botanical illustration is very precise. You must get every part of the plant just right. This takes a lot of attention to detail. Sometimes, I study a plant for hours. Only when I feel like I really 'know' the plant do I start drawing." —**Rusty Russell, former Botany Collections Manager of the National Herbarium**